LinkedIn Ads

revivalwaves

Published by RWG Publishing, 2021.

LINKEDIN ADS

First edition. August 2, 2021.

Written by revivalwaves.

Also by revivalwaves

Table of Contents

LinkedIn Ads

Welcome to this seminar on LinkedIn, publicizing. In this course, we will cover how to expand your scope with LinkedIn. This course is isolated into three modules. Module one covers beginning with crusade chief, module two covers making the real promotion, and module three covers focusing on and spending plans. When this course is finished, you'll realize how to successfully utilize LinkedIn commercials for your business. So right away, we should plunge into the principal module.

Module One

Welcome to module one. In this module, our specialists will tell you the best way to begin with crusade chief, so prepare to take a few notes, and how about we bounce directly in.

Okay, so we should begin with making our mission administrator account. Most importantly, what is the mission director record, and for what reason would you need one? A mission director account gives you admittance to lead-ins crusade administrator. The mission director instrument will then, at that point permit you to make promotions, similar to this. So you can promote on LinkedIn. Assuming you need to publicize on LinkedIn, you will require a mission administrator account. You can consider it a promoter's record.

Presently the cool thing about a mission chief record, is that it accompanies a customary record. You don't have to make another record. You simply need to sign into your LinkedIn profile, as I did here. This is only a common LinkedIn account. To make your mission chief record, simply click on the work, then, at that point promote.

Since I'm another publicist, LinkedIn needs some data before we can make my mission administrator account. The first is the record name, to assist you with distinguishing his record. As you can make numerous promotion accounts. The subsequent one is the money you will use to observe that this is lasting. You can't transform it once you say it, so watch out. Nonetheless, you can make a subsequent advertisement account with an alternate cash. In the event that you intend to utilize different monetary forms.

At long last, you can associate a LinkedIn page to your advertisement account, which is discretionary however strongly suggested, as it permits your promotion to show up in the newsfeed as supported substance, similar to this one.

Yet, until further notice, I won't interface a page. Wrap up by tapping on make account. So here's LinkedIn crusade chief. On the off chance that you've never utilized a comparative device it can look overpowering. So how about we separate it a piece. There are three principle tabs. The first is accounts. As you can have various advertisement accounts. The second is crusades, which you can't get to it without choosing an advertisement account. The third is promotions. Assuming you need to make another promotion account, simply click here on make account. Existing advertisement records will show up here. In the event that you have a great deal of promotion accounts, this rundown will be more populated. Presently, I just have one by drifting your cursor over the record name. You can either alter it...

Or then again audit its presentation.

Tapping on it will open up the mission bunches tab.

Mission bunches are only a way for you to coordinate your missions, it can keep things from going crazy, a mission gathering can have various organizations under it, and it's dependent upon you and how you need to structure your different missions. Here you can find that gathering name. The status, dynamic means you have empowered, however it's not running. It hasn't got a go sign for me, simply float your cursor in the little I symbol for more data. Here's the cash you spent on publicizing. Utilizing the money you chose, the impressions are how often the advertisement has been seen. Snaps, how often have individuals tapped on the promotion. The normal active clicking factor, normal expense per 1000 impressions, normal CPC, etc.

I trust you'll discover controls for penetrated on anything you need to discover. So for instance, I can simply see information from the previous 30 days, or from a particular reach.

What's more, I can likewise sort the information in slipping or rising way.

You can likewise send out this information as an accounting page, for additional examination. Simply click on send out. Select the information you need, and fare.

Consider these three tabs zooming in, going from something nonexclusive to more explicit. As recently referenced, a mission gathering will have at least one missions under it. A mission will have at least one promotions under it. Missions have similar controls as mission gatherings. So once more, you can sort by sliding or rising request.

You can apply channels. You can choose explicit date ranges.

Furthermore, you can look by crusade name, and you can look by crusade name in the event that you have a ton of missions.

Promotions are more established, basically the equivalent with pretty much sections.

Going up, you will discover site socioeconomics. This is like Google Analytics. This is like Google Analytics. It essentially uncovers insights about your site. Also, similar to Google

Analytics, you need to introduce something first before it opens up.

For this situation, they're considering it the Insight tag. Other than the site socioeconomics is the record resources. These are devices that are significant to making and overseeing advertisements on LinkedIn.

Furthermore, to wrap things up, the all inclusive image for settings, the stuff symbol. Tapping on it, we as of now redo a couple of things identifying with your record.

Goodness, and something last you need to charge card drawn advertisements on LinkedIn. That is the way you will pay them.

Furthermore, that is a short visit and outline of LinkedIn crusade supervisor. In the following video, we will make our first promotion. So thank you for watching and see you in the following one.

Module Two

Welcome to module two. In this module, our master will cover making the genuine advertisement. So prepare to take a few notes, and how about we bounce directly in.

We should begin with making a real LinkedIn. Thus, from the mission supervisor click on Create crusade here in the upper right, as everything begins with a mission.

Start by indicating where to bunch this mission, click on the Pencil symbol and pick where to put this under.

Furthermore, give your mission a decent name. You don't need it to be an untitled mission, as it's anything but an unmistakable title.

Okay, the principal thing you need to choose is the goal. What would you like to achieve with this mission? Is it mindfulness? Do you need more individuals to think about your business, or is it traffic, hits? Or on the other hand possibly you need more leads or site changes. This is a vital advance, and I recommend you take some time prior to choosing, as this will be the general objective of your mission. You're revealing to LinkedIn how you need your mission to be taken care of. All things considered, suppose I have another business. So right now, nobody thinks about it. Furthermore, I need some openness. So I picked brand mindfulness.

This is LinkedIn revealing to you how to deal with your mission. Your mission will be displayed to individuals well on the way to see your advertisements. What bodes well as my goal is to get openness for my new business. The following stop i the crowd. Who are individuals I need to see my promotion? So I click here in Audiences, and I can choose certain gatherings of individuals. So suppose my new business assists organization with recruiting the right contender for their employment opportunities. Every year may be a decent beginning.

After I've chosen my intended interest group, I need to pick an objective area. This doesn't matter to all advertisements, however we should see my new business will just take into account the Asian market. So I picked Asia.

I likewise have the choice to bar certain areas if necessary. So for instance, I don't need my promotion to be displayed in Latin America. So ensure it's rejected,

My promotion is in English, so I don't need to transform anything here. This is the place where you can be just about as nitty gritty as you need. Who is your intended interest group who are individuals you need to see your promotion. Snap on their crowd further to focus on specific individuals. Hearing crowd ascribes you can target individuals dependent on their organization's socioeconomics, similar to age or sexual orientation training, professional training, or interests. So how about we see I need individuals working in HR to see my promotion. So I click on Job Experience, then, at that point I click on Job Titles and type in, HR, and select HR director. These are largely the acceptable ideas, so I will add them.

You can perceive how incredible this apparatus is, as you can get as explicit as you need. It's additionally a smart thought to really have your optimal crowd as a main priority as you go through this. So for instance, suppose I need customers or from little to medium organizations as it were. So I add another necessity. Beside being HR. I additionally need individuals from little organizations. So I click on Narrow crowd further once more, in organization, organization size, perhaps 11 to 50 and afterward 51 to 200 workers.

Once more, I can reject certain individuals whenever required. Empower crowd development implies you need LinkedIn to naturally broaden your designated crowd on the off chance that it can't discover sufficient individuals. It is prescribed to keep this checked as people should your advertisement comes to as much as possible. In the event that you intend to utilize this crowd again for future missions. Snap on Save as layout, so you don't need to rehash this progression.

Before we proceed with making our promotion. We need to discuss the sorts of promotions that show up on LinkedIn. First is supported substance. This is an illustration of a supported advertisement. Also, it shows up on the newsfeed. This is likely the best kind of advertisement, as the possibility of somebody seeing it, and devouring the promotion is very high. The second are text advertisements. These are advertisements in text structure. Third, are supported in-mail advertisements. These are advertisements that show up in your message inbox. Another viable sort of an advertisement is a dis extremely immediate. In any case, be cautious as we have been adapted to disregard spam that shows up in our inboxes, similar to email. Fourth, our dynamic promotions or modified advertisements. These promotions will fluctuate with every individual. They're typically utilized for work enlisting and are very close to home. Fifth, our presentation promotions, there as picture structure.

Since we know the different sorts of LinkedIn advertisements. We can keep making our promotion design. This is the place where you pick what sort of advertisement you need. It very well may be a solitary picture advertisement, it very well may be a merry go round, or a progression of pictures, a video promotion or a video, a book advertisement, spotlight advertisement, or a devotee promotion. These three sorts will appear in the newsfeed. While text advertisements are as a rule in the upper right of the site. So suppose I will make a solitary picture advertisement. As referenced in a past video, particular kinds of advertisements require a LinkedIn organization page. This is the place where you put in the URL of that page, different advertisements like content promotions don't need an organization page. Do you take note of that relying upon the advertisement design? There will be highlights that are empowered or crippled, as for this situation. So how about we return to a solitary picture promotion. We are nearly done making our promotion, yet let us enjoy a reprieve here is that is a ton of data to process. So much obliged for watching. In the following video, we will wrap things up and finish our LinkedIn advertisement. See you there.

Module Three

Welcome to module three. In this module, our master will show you focusing on and advertisement spending plans. So prepare to take a few notes, and we should hop directly in.

How about we get from where we left off last time, and keep making our advertisement situation, LinkedIn Audience Network. The LinkedIn crowd organization, or spots outside the site where your promotion can show up, outsider accomplices off LinkedIn. I would suggest leaving this checked, as I said previously, the more individuals who see your advertisement, the better. Financial plan and timetable, spending plan, a day by day financial plan is what amount are you able to spend every day, while the all out financial plan is the amount they need to spend generally speaking. This is absolutely up to individual inclination. As I'm not mindful of your monetary imperatives or promoting.

Timetable, it is prescribed to pick the primary alternative, run crusade constantly from start date. The subsequent choice is for the most part utilized for advancements, when you start and end date, similar to a three-day deal for instance. Bid type, the suggested settings programmed bid, and let LinkedIn handle it. Change following. This is the point at which you need to know the number of changes these advertisements gone. What number of individuals purchased from your online store? The number of individuals pursue your pamphlet, etc. They click on close to go to the following page. Then, at that point click Save once more. Since we're finished making a mission. It's an ideal opportunity to add promotions to this mission. So click on Create new promotion.

This is the place where you transfer the picture of your advertisement. So click on Upload picture and pick your advertisement.

Type in an eye-getting feature, one that will make somebody quit looking over and read.

Type in a comparing depiction. When you stand out enough to be noticed with a feature, follow it up and mention to them what you need them to do.

The objective URL is the place where you need somebody to follow perusing your advertisement. This normally focuses to your own site.

On the right is the see sheet where you will perceive what your advertisement will resemble. Snap on the little circles beneath to perceive how your advertisement shows up in different structures.

When you're content with your promotion click on Create. Assuming you need to make more advertisements, simply click on Create new promotion here in the upper right corner. That subsequent promotion will show up underneath this first advertisement. You can likewise make changes to existing advertisements, by tapping on the three spots here, just as copy a promotion. On the off chance that you need to make a comparative advertisement with a couple of contrasts. On the right or the guage results. This is LinkedIn, most realistic estimation, and how your promotion will perform. As a matter of fact, this is about 90% exact. So you can utilize this as an aide and what things to change in your promotion for better outcomes. At the point when you're prepared, click on Launch Campaign to distribute your promotion. Furthermore, that is the manner by which you make a LinkedIn advertisement for your business. Once more, thank you for watching and I wish you accomplishment in promoting on LinkedIn.

Don't miss out!

Visit the website below and you can sign up to receive emails whenever revivalwaves publishes a new book. There's no charge and no obligation.

https://books2read.com/r/B-A-WNRB-LVXQB

BOOKS 2 READ

Connecting independent readers to independent writers.

Also by revivalwaves

About the Publisher

Accepting manuscripts in the most categories. We love to help people get their words available to the world.

Revival Waves of Glory focus is to provide more options to be published. We do traditional paperbacks, hardcovers, audio books and ebooks all over the world. A traditional royalty-based publisher that offers self-publishing options, Revival Waves provides a very author friendly and transparent publishing process, with President Bill Vincent involved in the full process of your book. Send us your manuscript and we will contact you as soon as possible.

Contact: Bill Vincent at rwgpublishing@yahoo.com www.rwgpublishing.com

www.ingramcontent.com/pod-product-compliance
Lightning Source LLC
Chambersburg PA
CBHW030537210326
41597CB00014B/1186